I0796114

CITY CRITTERS
Rabbits
by Betsy Rathburn
BLASTOFF! READERS
1
BELLWETHER MEDIA • MINNEAPOLIS, MN

Blastoff! Readers are carefully developed by literacy experts to build reading stamina and move students toward fluency by combining standards-based content with developmentally appropriate text.

LEVELS

Level 1 provides the most support through repetition of high-frequency words, light text, predictable sentence patterns, and strong visual support.

Level 2 offers early readers a bit more challenge through varied sentences, increased text load, and text-supportive special features.

Level 3 advances early-fluent readers toward fluency through increased text load, less reliance on photos, advancing concepts, longer sentences, and more complex special features.

★ **Blastoff! Universe**

Reading Level

Grade K

Grades 1–3

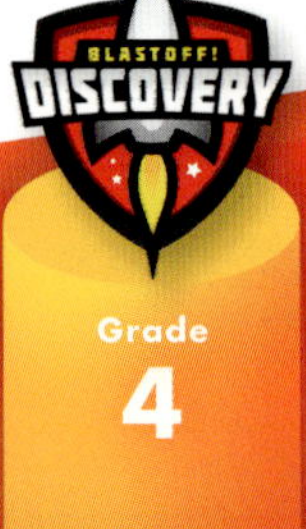

Grade 4

This edition first published in 2025 by Bellwether Media, Inc.

Library of Congress Cataloging-in-Publication Data

Names: Rathburn, Betsy, author.
Title: Rabbits / by Betsy Rathburn.
Description: Minneapolis, MN : Bellwether Media, 2025. | Series: Blastoff! Readers: City Critters | Includes bibliographical references and index. | Audience: Ages 5-8 | Audience: Grades K-1 | Summary: "Developed by literacy experts for students in kindergarten through grade three, this book introduces rabbits in cities to young readers through leveled text and related photos"– Provided by publisher.
Identifiers: LCCN 2024035390 (print) | LCCN 2024035391 (ebook) | ISBN 9798893042191 (library binding) | ISBN 9798893043167 (ebook)
Subjects: LCSH: Rabbits–Juvenile literature. | Urban animals–Juvenile literature.
Classification: LCC QL737.L32 R378 2025 (print) | LCC QL737.L32 (ebook) | DDC 599.32–dc23/eng/20240810
LC record available at https://lccn.loc.gov/2024035390
LC ebook record available at https://lccn.loc.gov/2024035391

Editor: Christina Leaf   Designer: Gabriel Hilger

Printed in the United States of America, North Mankato, MN.

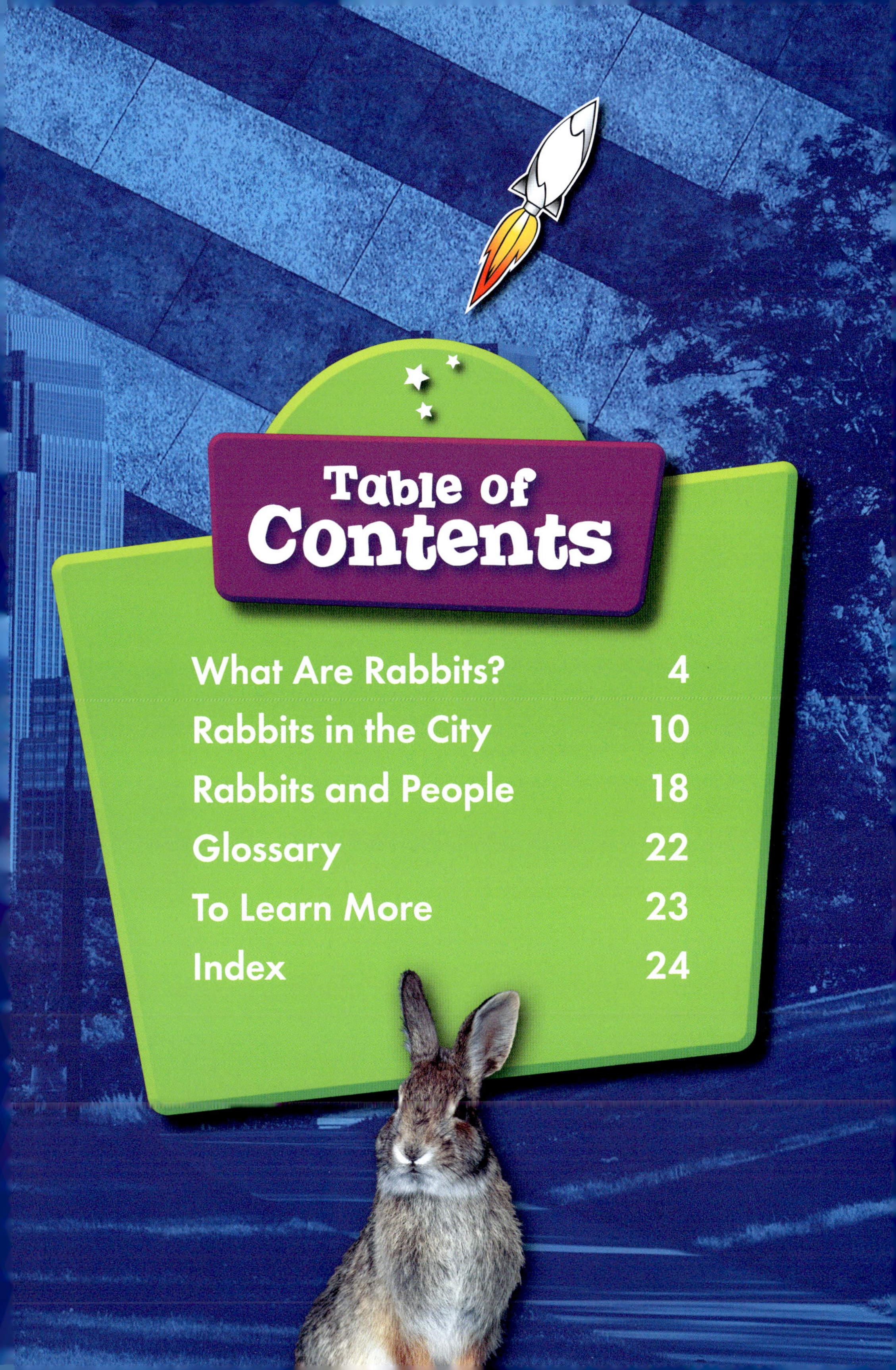

Table of Contents

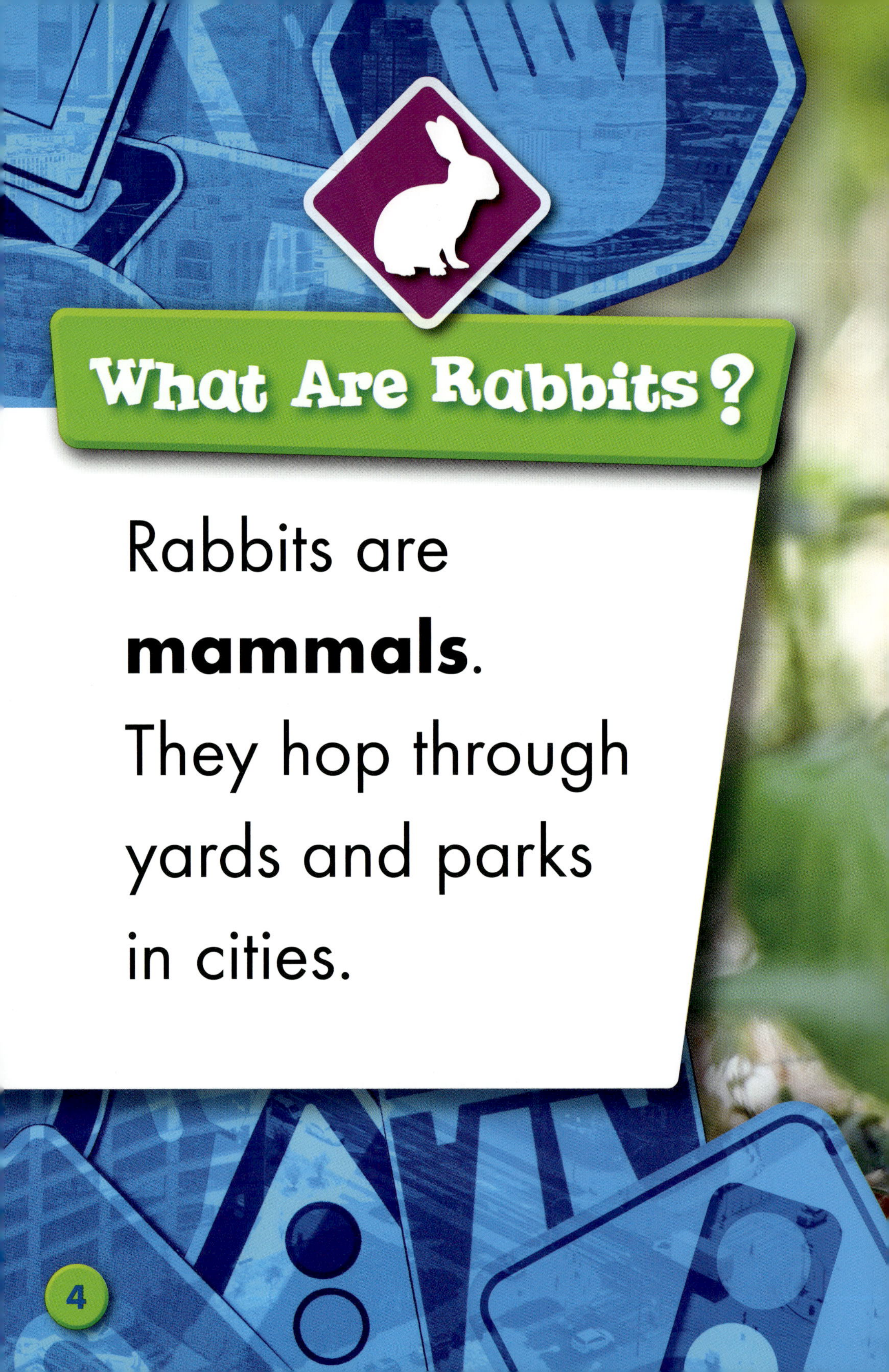

What Are Rabbits?

Rabbits are **mammals**. They hop through yards and parks in cities.

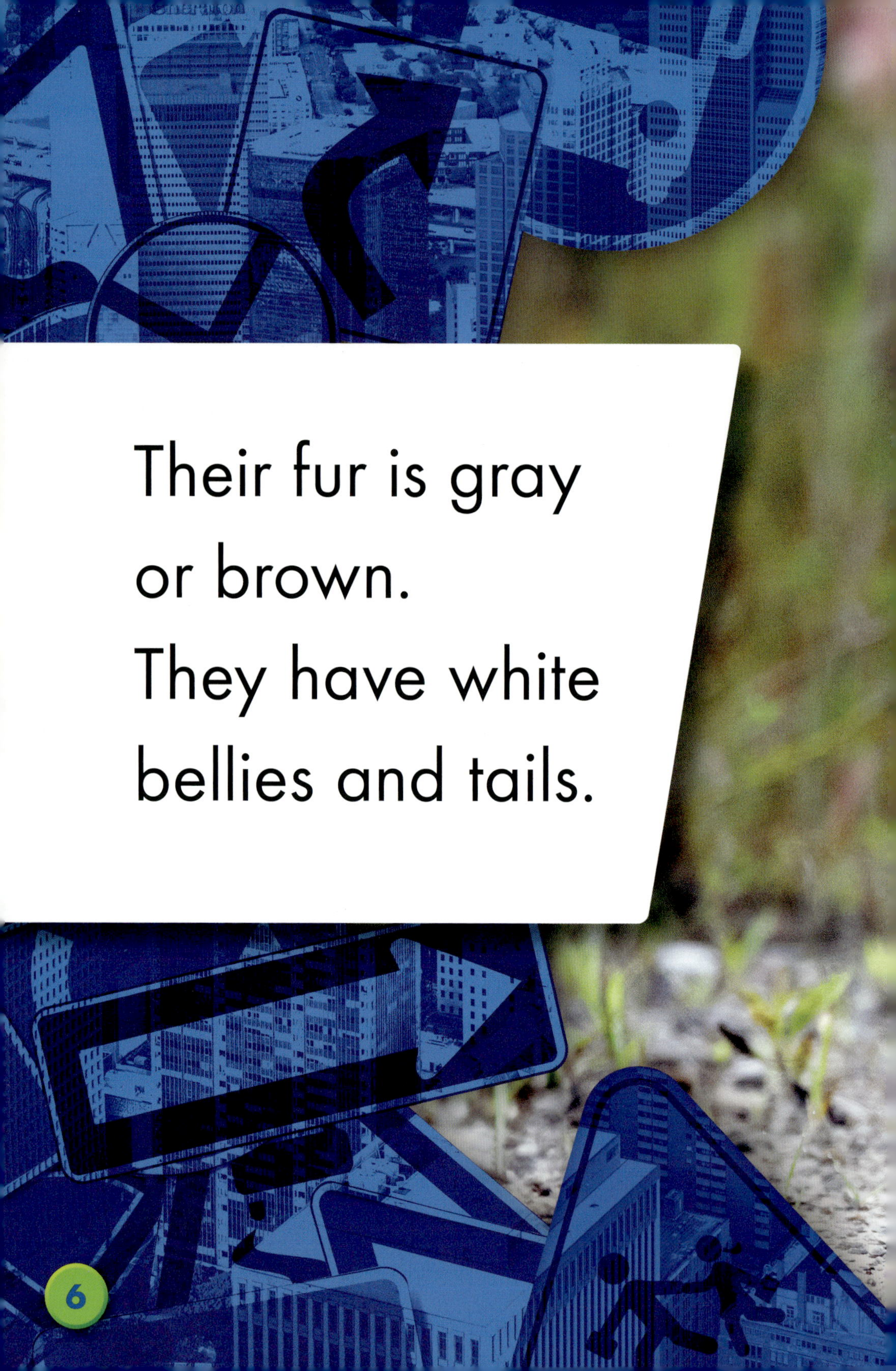

Their fur is gray
or brown.
They have white
bellies and tails.

Common City Rabbit
eastern cottontail
tail

They have long ears.
Big back feet
help them run fast.

back feet
ears

Rabbits in the City

Rabbits live alone. They hide among grass and **shrubs**.

Rabbit Homes
grass
shrubs
holes

They come out around sunrise and sunset. They look for food.

They eat grass, fruits, and vegetables. In winter, they eat sticks and **bark**.

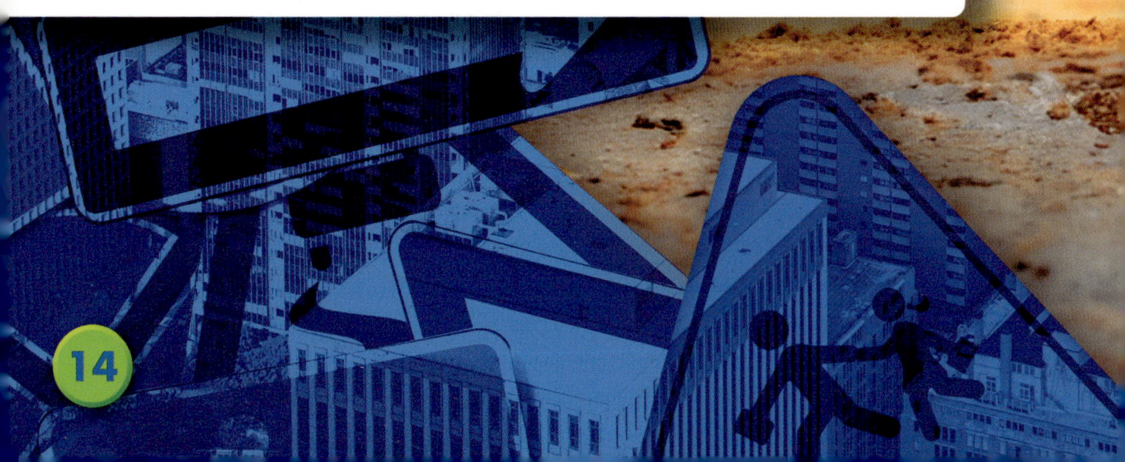

Rabbit Food
grass
vegetables
bark

Rabbits are **alert**. They stand to listen for danger. They run from **predators** and people.

predator

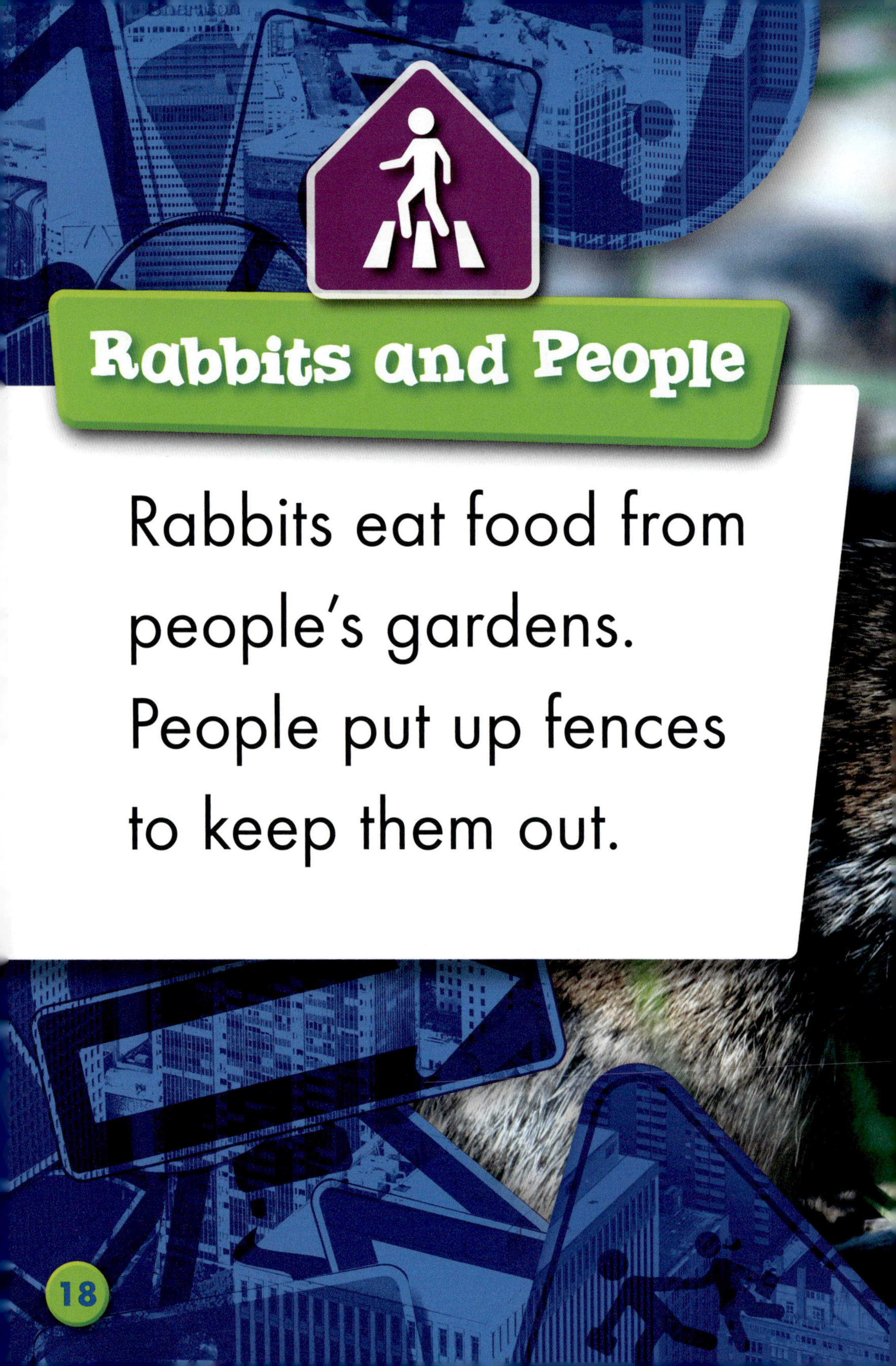

Rabbits and People

Rabbits eat food from people's gardens. People put up fences to keep them out.

fence

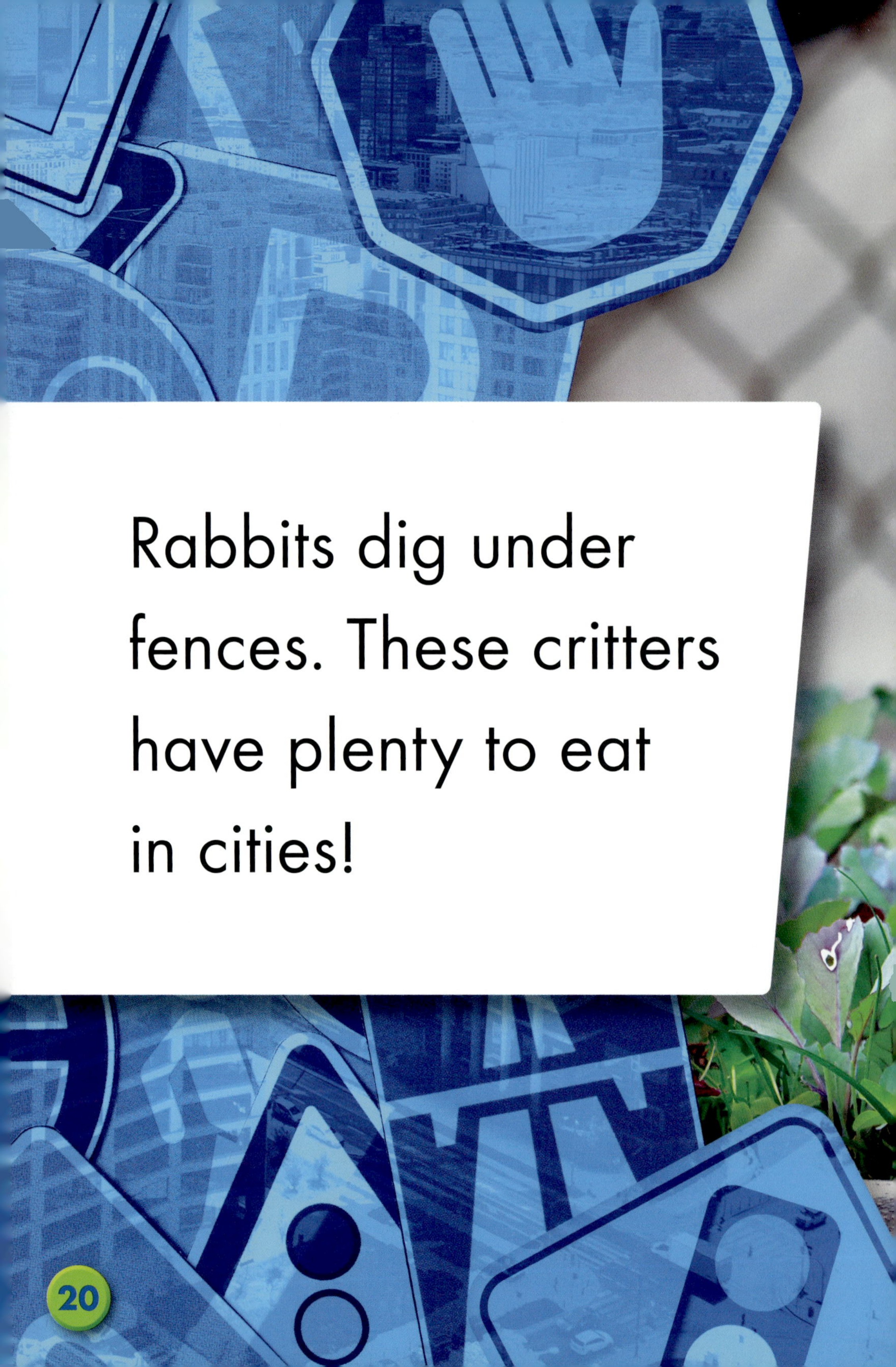

Rabbits dig under fences. These critters have plenty to eat in cities!

Glossary

alert

quick to notice danger

predators

animals that hunt other animals for food

bark

the hard covering of trees

shrubs

bushes

mammals

warm-blooded animals that have backbones and feed their young milk

To Learn More

AT THE LIBRARY

Chanez, Katie. *Rabbit Kits in the Wild.* Minneapolis, Minn.: Jump!, 2024.

Leaf, Christina. *Rabbit or Hare?* Minneapolis, Minn.: Bellwether Media, 2020.

McDonald, Amy. *Rabbits.* Minneapolis, Minn.: Bellwether Media, 2021.

ON THE WEB

FACTSURFER

Factsurfer.com gives you a safe, fun way to find more information.

1. Go to www.factsurfer.com.
2. Enter "rabbits" into the search box and click 🔍.
3. Select your book cover to see a list of related content.

Index

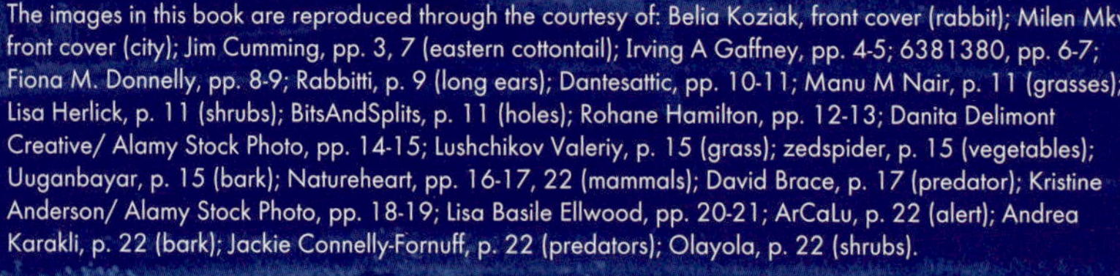

The images in this book are reproduced through the courtesy of: Belia Koziak, front cover (rabbit); Milen Mkv, front cover (city); Jim Cumming, pp. 3, 7 (eastern cottontail); Irving A Gaffney, pp. 4-5; 6381380, pp. 6-7; Fiona M. Donnelly, pp. 8-9; Rabbitti, p. 9 (long ears); Dantesattic, pp. 10-11; Manu M Nair, p. 11 (grasses); Lisa Herlick, p. 11 (shrubs); BitsAndSplits, p. 11 (holes); Rohane Hamilton, pp. 12-13; Danita Delimont Creative/ Alamy Stock Photo, pp. 14-15; Lushchikov Valeriy, p. 15 (grass); zedspider, p. 15 (vegetables); Uuganbayar, p. 15 (bark); Natureheart, pp. 16-17, 22 (mammals); David Brace, p. 17 (predator); Kristine Anderson/ Alamy Stock Photo, pp. 18-19; Lisa Basile Ellwood, pp. 20-21; ArCaLu, p. 22 (alert); Andrea Karakli, p. 22 (bark); Jackie Connelly-Fornuff, p. 22 (predators); Olayola, p. 22 (shrubs).